INFLUENCERS

The Future Belongs to You

Dr. Travis C. Jennings

Dedication

This manuscript is dedicated to every *emerging influencer* in the kingdom. The world is changing and will soon look quite differently than it does now.

But the future belongs to the INFLUENCER – so we're in great hands.

Table of Contents

Introduction

The advent of social media has created an entire world and subculture of information, connectivity, and interconnectivity. Some would argue that it has now positioned itself to become the driving force of our society in some manner. Fortune 500 companies are now spending millions and billions of dollars competing for social media strategists to help them create campaigns ensuring their brands can compete and survive in an ever-changing, global climate. These companies are hoping to get ahead of their competitors or even just merely remain relevant. Spokespersons for these large brands were the celebrities of old like the Chicago Bulls' Michael Jordan for *Nike* , the rap group RUN DMC for Addidas or even Bill Cosby for the world famous JELL-O; which many of us can recall the catchy jingle that became lodged in our memories. Many of these celebrities of old have either simply gotten old or fallen into scandals of their own.

Companies and brands (both new and old) have had to reshape and restructure the way they market. The rise of social media as a viable outlet for reaching traditional and non-traditional consumers has changed the entire marketing landscape. Consequently, the newest type of "spokesperson" or brand champion or for the sake of this manuscript – *influencer* is no longer limited to celebrities. Because these companies understand the importance of social media, they have incorporated strategies that allow them to align themselves with

Introduction
(cont'd)

specific social media tactics for reaching both their non-traditional and traditional consumers directly.

These social media influencers and their followers hold the key to some brands' eventual and overall successes. When thinking about the revelation of *Influencers*, it was easy to understand why influencers are so important and timely for the kingdom and its advancement. If we are going to continue to push the kingdom's agenda in the coming times, then we are going to have to embrace the revelation of the INFLUENCER.

I was burdened with the coming generation's capability to keep the purpose and potency of the gospel in tact, impacting, and moving in a society whose ideals and culture are rapidly changing. Ultimately, this manuscript has been created to speak to the heart of every emerging influencer in each sector (mountain) of influence.

The future belongs to the influencer and it's time to change the world.

Chapter 1
WHAT IS AN INFLUENCER?

Matthew 5:13-16: Ye are the salt of the earth: but if the salt have lost his savour, wherewith shall it be salted? it is thenceforth good for nothing, but to be cast out, and to be trodden under foot of men. Ye are the light of the world. A city that is set on an hill cannot be hid. Neither do men light a candle, and put it under a bushel, but on a candlestick; and it giveth light unto all that are in the house. Let your light so shine before men, that they may see your good works, and glorify your Father which is in heaven.

The Bible tells us that God does nothing in the earth, *except He reveals it to his servants the prophets (Amos 3:7).* Here is the revelation: When God wants to get something into the earth, He will raise up men to use as the avenue for executing His will in the earth.

We can see all throughout the Bible where He has used men to execute His agenda. We're not referring to gender only, but we are specifically referring to men in position. When God wanted wisdom in the earth, He raised up Solomon. When God wanted to spare His people from the flood, He raised up Noah. When God wanted praise to be released in the earth, He raised up David. When God wanted to save mankind from their sins He raised up Jesus.

Anytime God wants to transact something in the earth, He will raise up someone, somewhere to perform what He needs them to do. God is about to raise somebody up! Anytime God wants to do something in the earth, He will always raise up someone, to decree and to declare His agenda. So anytime God raises up an apostolic or a prophetic voice, He does so because there is a revelation He is attempting to get to you.

Revelation is revealed knowledge. The Bible says, my people perish for the lack of knowledge. Because they perish for the lack of knowledge, there is revelation God wants to give us but sometimes we are not are in the right position to receive this revelation. Why? **Because you can only go as far as your revelation.** When Moses received revelation that he was more than Pharoah's son, he helped to free over a million slaves from Pharoah's bondage. When Joshua received revelation that he was more than the son of Nun, he moved into succession and he began to help bring the people of God out of the wilderness and into the Promise Land.

When Esther received revelation that she was more than an orphan girl, she stepped into **queenship.**

When Nehemiah received revelation that he was not just a prophet, but he was also a political figure with the authority speak to powers, he rebuilt the broken down walls of Jerusalem. When David received revelation that he was more than a shepherd boy, he helped to usher the glory of God back into Israel. So believer, you don't really need more money right now, what you really need is a revelation. Revelation is about to explode over your life! You cannot be hindered when you have a revelation. You cannot be sabotaged when you have a revelation. **You cannot be rejected or abandoned when you have a revelation.**

Psalm 27:10-11 declares that *when my mother and father forsake me, then the Lord will take me up.* Therefore, when they leave you, God's going to lift you. When they try to break you, then you have to know that God's getting ready to bless you. When you have revelation that you cannot be cursed in a season like this, they are going to try and curse you, but they are going to have to bless you instead. Guess what? God has shifted the assignment of your enemies! Your enemy's assignment was to try and kill you, but now God has shifted it and now they are going to bless you!

Say this: God has just shifted the assignment of my enemies!

* * * * * * *

11

I performed an interesting demonstration during one Sunday morning service. I chose a random group of people and separated them into three groups. I had the ushers hand one group a pack of unsalted peanuts. To the second group, we gave them salted peanuts; and to the last group, we gave them slightly sweetened peanuts. We did the same thing with another set of people and used oatmeal instead of peanuts. With each group, I asked them to be as honest and expressive as possible concerning the taste of their samples. Then I asked them to use one-word descriptors to communicate what they were experiencing as they ate their samples. Some of the words the unsalted sample group used were: dry, bland, basic, pasty and even disgusting. The words used by the salted group were: full of flavor. No surprise here.

We had the other group perform the same exercise with their oatmeal samples. The same thing happened. Their responses and facial expressions were consistent with the previous group's responses. However, in this example, there was one person who absolutely did not want to take another bite of the bland oatmeal. She actually frowned, while the other group completely devoured the sweetened oatmeal.

In both instances of the peanuts and the oatmeal and our sample subjects, the product remained the same; however, the difference in flavor is what yielded the myriad of responses. There were notable, positive responses and just as many notable and negative responses when the "flavor" of our sample product did not suit the tastes of our sample group.

INFLUENCERS

Just like our demonstration, we have the same common denominator, but a different flavor. The point here is that for those individuals who have earned a certain amount on your job, in your career, or in your business. You have hit a plateau and you are wondering what can you do now to break the glass ceiling you are facing? Perhaps it is not the common denominator that should change, but perhaps it's your flavor? Maybe it's time to consider changing your flavor? Your flavor is about to SHIFT and God is about turn you into an INFLUENCER!

Yes, something is about to fall upon you that is going to cause people to see you and cause them to be affected by you. God is about to shift your whole game up! **Say this: Hello, my name is Influencer!**

Remember Influencer, not everyone will grasp this revelation. But for the ones that are hungry enough, wear it on your chest like I asked people to do during one morning's service while releasing this *Influencers* message. That morning, we literally passed out "Hello, My Name Is..." stickers to everyone present. We asked everyone to write "INFLUENCER" in the space that asked for the name. Everyone followed suit and I asked them to place the sticker on their chest. In that moment, everyone's name was supernaturally changed to INFLUENCER.

Therefore, in *Matthew 5:13, it declares that you are the salt of the earth, but if the salt has lost his savor wherefore, shall it be salted? It is thenceforth good for nothing but to be cast out and to be trodden upon the foot of me and we are the light of the world. A city that is set on a hill, that cannot be hidden. Neither do men light a candle and put it under a bushel, but on a candle stand or candlestick and it gives illumination and to all that are in the house. Let your light so shine before men that they may see your good works and glorify the father, which is in heaven.* In this manuscript, I want to release to you the revelation of *kingdom influencers.*

Influencer is not a word I created. When you Google the word "influencers," you will note that there are many types of influencers. One influencer type is a marketing influencer. There are individuals on social media that are very engaging with their audiences and are very interactive with the people that follow them on social media within their various accounts. When this happens, major companies like Nike, Addidas, Starbucks, and etc., may take notice. These companies may offer to pay these social media influencers to promote their product or services among their followers by simply posting information about their various brands within within their accounts.

* * * * * *

So what is an influencer? An Influencer is an individual who has the capacity to have an effect on the character development or behavior of someone or something. Someone who affects or changes the way other people behave. For example, let's look at the actress Selena Gomez, the singer Ariana Grande, Taylor Swift, The "Rock", Beyonce and even Oprah just to name a few.

If Beyonce or Oprah were to touch something, take a picture with, or mention a certain product or service, within 24 hours, the stock of that product or service would likely increase.

People can say what they will about the Kardashians, but they have made hundreds of millions of dollars without any talent. They can't dance, they can't sing, but they understand contracts. The Kardashians understand that they are a brand and they have strategically capitalized on their brand. They have generated millions of dollars because they've mastered the art of "influencing" and have coupled that with their social media reach.

We've heard about social media influencers. We've heard about marketing influencers, but now God is releasing a revelation upon kingdom influencers that everywhere these influencers walk, they will have the capability to bring an effect upon characters and behaviors. You are about to affect change at your job, in your community, in your church and in your family. A person that has influence is a person who has the power to influence people through social media as well as traditional media. They have the ability to affect traits and temperaments.

Guess what influencer? You're, getting ready to affect the traits and temperaments of people you felt were a lost cause. People that were in a rebellious state, a deplorable state, a hopeless and even a reprobate state are going to have a change of heart and a change of mind because you are in their lives. You are about to change behaviors and temperaments.

15

Not only will you be able to change traits and temperaments, but also you'll have the ability to affect mentalities and mannerisms – all because you showed up. Atmospheres and environments will shift because the influencer showed up. People that were set to curse you are now going to start blessing you.

* * * * * *

The best thing that ever happened to your family was when you showed up. The reason why God's not going to destroy your bloodline is because you are a bloodline changer. The reason why God's not going to destroy your lineage is because YOU were born in that lineage. You were exactly what your lineage needed. **Say this: That's why the enemy tried to destroy me.** Why? Because the enemy knew that an influencer was coming. He knew that someone who has the ability to affect traits, temperaments, mentality, mannerisms, attitudes AND activities was coming. Influencer, there is grace, genius, and greatness on the inside of you, that God is going to take to the next level!

When I first came into the kingdom, I didn't believe Christians could have millions. I didn't believe that Christians could live a life full of joy, peace, and happiness. In the church I came from, we were all "climbing up the rough side of the mountain!" But I also had to connect to other influencers in order learn and develop a culture that allowed me and the others I lead to believe that *NOW unto him that is able to do exceeding abundantly above all that I can ever ask or think (Ephesians 3:20)!*

Influencers Need Agility

As an influencer, it's important to have **agility.** Agility is the ability to move quickly and easily; with fluidity. It is the POWER to be able to move swiftly. Therefore, what has not happened for you previously, will now happen and it will happen quickly because of the power of agility. You will also have the power to even understand and comprehend quickly; along with the power to be clever. You will have the power to be a solutionist – someone or some group that solves problems.

You see influencer, the reason why most people spent so much time in their perversion was because they had not yet realized their purpose. **Any man who doesn't know his purpose, will spend more time in his perversion.** Some still have a same-sex attraction issue, a lying issue or an adultery issue. Why? Because when a man is still in the dark about is who he is and his ability, then he will continue to act like a dog in heat. But when a man finds out he was actually created in the image and the likeness of God, then he will run towards his purpose and leave his perversion alone.

Say this: I'm an influencer. I'm an influencer. I'm an influencer. I AM an influencer!

Consider this: every 15 seconds, commercials are influencing you. You don't even wear *Depends* undergarments. But because the girl in the commercial is so likable, you're influenced to believe that maybe you do need a pack of

Depends – if just for a moment. But that is marketing; you are constantly saturated with advertisements so your behaviors, perceptions and perspectives are influenced to eventually make a purchase. Guess what? Your agility is going to the next level and your genius is about to saturate your market.

* * * * * *

There are *biblical influencers, secular influencers,* and there are *also sacred influencers.* Let's take a look at a few sacred influencers:

In 1 Samuel, first chapter, there was Hannah. She was a **prayerful influencer.** Then there was Esther. She was a **prominent influencer.** In John the 4th chapter, the woman at the well is a **progressive influencer.** Looking at 2 Samuel, verse 14 at David, we see that David is a **passionate influencer.** In 1 Kings 17, we see that Elijah is a **prophetic influencer.** In Nehemiah 6:17, we see Nehemiah as a **political influencer.** Influencers are just as relevant now as they were all throughout the scriptures.

Then there's Jesus. Jesus is the *greatest* influencer. Peter, James, and John were all at the lake, washing their nets. These are professionals that had been active in their professions for over 25 years. They knew everything there was to know about fishing; logistically and technically speaking. They understood the best time of day for fishing, where to find the most fish, what type of bait to use and etc. They are well informed about the game of fishing and they were likely in their mid-fifties. Suddenly, this young gentleman by the name of Jesus walks by as if He's going to pass them.

Jesus was walking by and noticed that what they were doing was not effective and said, "hey, follow me!" They dropped their nets and they began to follow Him. This was a very important act. *They dropped their nets and they followed.* Could it be that something you're doing is not as effective as it could be? That maybe something you're doing is not adding up to your destiny and your purpose and Jesus is saying, "Okay, it doesn't matter how long you've been doing that. Are, you ready to drop what you're doing and follow me; follow my guidance and instruction?" That's the power of influence, to cause people to drop their assignment(s) and connect to yours.

Say this: I am not out of ideas. I am not out of vision, I am not out of purpose. I'm not even out of potential, but I am out of partners. I need someone to assist and connect to me to bring my vision to pass!

That's what Jesus exemplified. His influence caused men to drop what they were doing and follow Him. Do you have what Jesus had? The Bible tells us *that greater is he that's in me than he that is in the world (1John 4:4).* It also declares *that I can do all things through Christ that strengthens me (Philippians 4:13). It's Christ in me, the hope of all of these glorious things (Colossians 1:27).* So what's been convincing you that you don't have the right juice? What's been convincing you that you don't

19

have enough Jesus? Lastly, who's been convincing you that you don't have the right jump?

Influencer, you need to tell them that they are inaccurate and they have been misinformed because you have been made in the image of God and after the likeness of God. God didn't say, I am only going to give Adam dominion; no, He said that I have given dominion to both male and female. There is a dominion authority that has been lying dormant on the inside of you. NOW is the time to activate it. **Say this: I HAVE the right juice, I have enough jump, and I have enough Jesus for my assignment!**

* * * * * *

You must understand that you have a mantle that is greater than all of your mistakes. You have a mantle that is greater than all of your mishaps. You have a mantle on you that is greater than all of your misunderstandings and mishandlings. Now influencer, you're getting ready to bring impact to your family, your city, your region, and the world.

The Bible says that you are the salt of the earth and you are the light of the world. Aren't you curious about what Jesus is conveying? He is saying here that salt influences darkness. He is saying that you, influencer, are the salt of the earth. The earth means the region. You are the salt of the region and you are the salt of your country. You are the salt of the soil, you are the salt of the ground, and you are also the light of the world.

Now, "world" in this context means the cosmos or beyond the world as we know it; the universe. The Bible says that we wrestle not against flesh and blood, but against principalities, against powers, the rulers of darkness of this world, spiritual wickedness in high places. Influencer, you are the salt in your region.

* * * * * * *

INFLUENCER DECLARATIONS

I **decree and declare** that you are an influencer. You affect and change temperaments and mindsets because of your genius, your grace and your greatness.

I **decree and declare** that you are the motivator. You have been given a grace to influence others to reach their purpose in destiny.

I **decree and declare** that you are an enforcer. You make things happen and you get things done!

I **decree and declare** that you are the salt AND the light; you bring the favor AND the flavor!

I **decree and declare** that you have been created and commissioned to bring change!

Chapter 2
APOSTOLIC INFLUENCERS

An **influencer** is an individual that has the capacity to have an effect on character development and behaviors. An **influencer** is someone or something that can also affect change. *My* definition of an influencer is someone who has the ability to affect traits, mentality, mannerisms, attitudes and even activities. **Influencers** have the ability to literally shift how people think and how people act.

In the 1500's, there was a monk by the name of Martin Luther. He was living in a monastery and he had learned that other priests were selling pardons. Let me explain. During this time, there was major work that needed to be done on the structure of the temples and different religious houses. In order to generate income for the repairs, the priests decided to charge people who were in need of repentance. As Martin Luther studied, he read in Romans that according to the Word of God, we are justified by faith; which means we are already righteous before God. Therefore, we don't have to pay for repentance because Jesus already paid the ultimate sacrifice. In light of this truth, Martin Luther nailed a 95-page thesis on the front door of the church outlining what he had learned. With this act, he stood against the hypocrisy of the church and against what the church was doing at that particular time. **Say this: someone has to stand up!**

* * * * * * *

Many are connected to our ministry and many are connected to other ministries that are similar in nature – progressive, cutting-edge and relevant. If you are covered by your ministry and have submitted to the curriculum of your ministry, you are **apostolic**. The word apostolic does not mean we wear veils atop our heads while we "quicken" and "shake." No, no, no – that's tradition. It is quite likely that you are the first in your family to be connected to a ministry movement that is considered apostolic. During a Wednesday night bible study, I asked our congregation to raise their hand if they were the first in their family to be connected to an apostolic ministry and over 75% of the people that were in attendance that night raised their hands.

You have planted, you have pioneered, and you have embraced the process. Therefore, you are creating a path that others will walk. That's why your word, your witness and your warfare in your life has been intense. You have had to face what other apostolic influencers had to face and YOU WILL WIN in the end. So stop doubting and let's make it official. You are an apostolic influencer. **Say this: I'm not going to doubt this again. I know who I am. I believe in planting. I believe in pioneering. I absolutely believe in the process and that makes me an apostolic influencer!**

You are likely the first in your family to have an influencer and an apostolic mindset. You are probably the first in your family who has been challenged to walk in this level of faith and even the first in your family even to speak the truth with power. You have been looking for a prototype but this is why you can't find an example because **YOU ARE the prototype**. You are the apostolic influencer – because you are the first.

If you are connected, covered, and submitted to a ministry's apostolic curriculum, then you are apostolic. Covered is different from connected. A lot of people are connected, but they are not covered. What does this mean? You have been given an assignment it, but you still do what you want to do. You don't seek out any type of apostolic deliberation or any type of apostolic oversight or counsel, you just do what you want to do, but you're still a member of the church. True submission is not just connection, but it is also covering. I should also run my kingdom assignments through a system or protocol that allows someone to review, judge, critique, and give insight on.

If you're doing anything without being "sent," you're illegitimate. This is why what you are doing may never go to the nations, because God will never release *bastards* into the kingdom. *John 3:16 says, For God so loved the world that he gave his only begotten son.* Therefore, this proves that God is releasing son into the world, **not bastards.**

Apostolic Curriculum

Years ago, during one Bible Study service, I started a prophetic teaching about "Champions: it's time to get in the ring." Prior to this day, we (our ministry) had never heard a definition like "champions are those that fight the good fight of faith. Who win over every attack of satan with unwavering stamina. They are warriors who defend and uphold the integrity of the Word of God." This *one* revelation turned into a book and that book paid for my daughter's college education and she graduated debt free. Champions was an *apostolic curriculum* that attempted to convey a necessary revelation to the people of God. It changed mindsets with the revelation that declared that you are not a wimp, but you are a champion.

Another time came into service and declared that the Lord wanted us to go back to His "original plan" and because we are going back to the original plan, we are "Reformers." This is what Martin Luther was. He was a reformer. Sometimes the church can deviate from the original blueprint handed to them from God. For example: Your mother, your mother's mother and her mother have been successfully baking cakes for over three decades. Then you come along and because you're vegan, you decide to use pumpkin seeds instead of eggs. What do you think they would say if they were to taste your vegan cake? **Someone has deviated from the blueprint.**

Deliverance was always in our nature (kingdom). Breakthrough was in our nature. Every time we came together, signs, wonders, and miracles manifested. What happened? The church as a whole has slowly deviated from God's original blueprint for kingdom. Now, God's desire is to bring the church back to His original blueprint so that we are no longer performers, but we are now reformers. We are becoming a people that will take a stand even when everyone else is sitting down. We have the attitude that when everyone else bows down to false idols, we are standing up and are saying Jehovah is God. Jesus is our God.

So these apostolic curricula are now implemented in regions like the south where there is a strong activity of witchcraft, wizardry, warlocks, and Wicca (an organized term [religion] for the practice of an arm of witchcraft, sorcery and other pagan rituals).

Now, most of us have entered into and connected to ministries where we hear and discover things that we have never heard and because your lineage may be rooted in witchcraft and rebellion, the first thing you will likely say is "let me check this or I don't believe that because I've never heard that before."

TRAVIS C. JENNINGS

However, because you have never heard something before does not mean it is not in the scriptures. Because you have never heard that "obedience is better than sacrifice," doesn't mean it is not in the scriptures. An **Apostolic Curriculum** changes minds, perspectives, and lives.

There was another time I had begun teaching on the concept of metrons. I'd never heard of a metron, prior to reading about it in scripture. When Paul began to tell other followers not to compare him to another man's measure, another man's boundary, or another man's territory in *Corinthians*. He says, "I know my measure and I know my metron."

Paul in this text also said, "I'm not going to reach beyond my metron." Going *beyond* your metron is how frustration creeps in. Have you ever felt frustrated? Have you ever felt so frustrated that you were spinning your wheels, but you weren't making any traction, movement or progress? Could it be that you were just working outside of your metron or your sphere of grace? Every metron has a grace. What is the grace of God? The grace of God is more than what you do before you eat your food. *The grace of God is the enabling power of God to help you complete your assignment(s).*

* * * * * *

So these apostolic curricula are more than just the story of Daniel in some type of lion's den – that is not going to set you free or change your mindset entirely. But now I'd like to continue with the revelation of another influencer type: **apostolic influencers**.

* * * * * * *

The term apostle comes from the word *apostolos*, which means one who is sent or one that sends. *1 Corinthians 12: 28, And God hath set some in the church, first apostles, secondarily prophets, thirdly teachers.* Pastors are not even mentioned in this text because pastors are not the foundation of the church. The foundation of the church are apostles, prophets, then teachers and after that, the working of miracles. Could it be the reason that we aren't seeing miracles is because the church is out of order? You would never insert money into a vending machine when there is a huge sign slapped on it that says "out of order."

If you are an administrator of an apostolic house, then you are likely to have great warfare just like the biblical apostles encountered because the administration of an apostolic house has to be equal or greater strength than the apostles, the prophets and the teacher. Why? Because the apostle is one that governs. The prophet is one that guides and the teacher is the one that grounds. So the apostle is going to establish what God is saying, but it is the administration that must make sense out of everything that God gives the apostles and they must execute. This is why the enemy is after those that assist apostles.

First in Rank

Apostolic also means first in rank. Apostles have been sent in the church by God and "first" in this instance means proton or first in importance and order. Apostles cultivate you from a raw state. They begin to develop you and in that development God begins to deploy you. A pastor doesn't have the grace for this part of the process. A pastor can only shepherd. They cannot push you into destiny – unless that pastor has an apostolic "push." Apostles are first in importance and order.

Acts 13:2 says, *As they ministered to the Lord, and fasted, the Holy Ghost said, Separate me Barnabas and Saul for the work whereunto I have called them.* This verse tells us that it was the time for the apostles to be separated and sent into apostolic ministry. God sent Barnabas and Saul out through the apostles. So, at this particular time James was over the church and he sent out Saul and Barnabas. This also confirms that if you are sent without an apostolic release, then you are **illegitimate.** *Matthew 10:5 says, these twelve Jesus sent forth, and commanded them, saying, Go not into the way of the Gentiles, and into any city of the Samaritans enter ye not;* we're still talking about apostolic influencers. Jesus sent forth these twelve and commanded them to go.

1 Corinthians 4:15 says, *for though you have 10,000 instructors in Christ yet have you not have many fathers for in Christ Jesus I have begotten you.* This is the Apostle Paul. He said, you have the seal of my apostleship.

Therefore, before God makes you an influencer, He will first connect you with another apostolic influencer who will help develop you. **An apostle won't leave you on the table to die.** He will nurture you and then he will push you and your assignment. He'll also see you when you fall and when you fall or fall short and he's right there to help you up and get you back on your path of destiny.

Who are Apostles?

Who are apostles? What do they do? They are **fathers**. They are **pioneers**, they **launch**, and they **empower**. They **teach**. They **ground**. An apostle does not have traditional sermons; however, he walks in revelation. Apostles will keep teaching on a revelation until it leaves his spirit. God will download daily bread into the belly of apostolic and prophetic people and now there is a "window" for somebody, a person, a place, a thing to pray out or intercede about. This download may even need to be released in the form of a decree, declaration or an *apostolic curriculum*. However, if apostolic and prophetic people hold on to that download without expressing it or releasing it and they take it into their tomorrow, the next week, or even the next year, it may turn into maggots. It is similar to what God did for the children of Israel in Exodus. He said that he would give them daily bread, but He also warned them not to have any leftovers. **Say this: I will not have any leftovers in my belly!**

31

THE INFLUENCER APOSTOLIC PUSH

I **decree and declare** that your immobile days are over.

I **decree and declare** that your stuck days are over and I **decree and declare** that there is a divine push that's hitting you in the spirit. In the name of Jesus!

I **decree and declare** the release of visions, dreams, abilities, anointings and talents on the inside of this influencer that have been lying dormant. **Father, right now, I shake them up in the spirit!**

I **decree** that resurrection power now hits their bellies. Nothing on the inside of them will be dormant, but they will move into activation and activate, activate, activate!

Father, we decree activation now!

Chapter 3
THE IDENTITY OF AN INFLUENCER

Jeremiah 1:4-10 reads, *Then the word of the Lord came unto me, saying,Before I formed thee in the belly I knew thee; and before thou camest forth out of the womb I sanctified thee, and I ordained thee a prophet unto the nations. Then said I, Ah, Lord God! behold, I cannot speak: for I am a child. But the Lord said unto me, Say not, I am a child: for thou shalt go to all that I shall send thee, and whatsoever I command thee thou shalt speak. Be not afraid of their faces: for I am with thee to deliver thee, saith the Lord. Then the Lord put forth his hand, and touched my mouth. And the Lord said unto me, Behold, I have put my words in thy mouth. See, I have this day set thee over the nations and over the kingdoms, to root out, and to pull down, and to destroy, and to throw down, to build, and to plant*

The Influencer's Call

A little background on Jeremiah: He was a the son of a prophet named Hilkiah who was a Hebrew high priest at the time of King Josiah. His name is mentioned in II Kings. He was known for finding a lost copy of the Book of the Law at the Temple in Jerusalem at the time that King Josiah commanded that the temple be refurbished. Jeremiah comes from the Benjamite village so Jeremiah came from a village whose name means the right hand of God. In Lamentations and in the book of Jeremiah, the Prophet Jeremiah always had the massive burden of warning Israel because of their continuous acts of sins against God. The Bible goes on to tell us that the Jews had now slipped into adultery and they had stopped worshipping Jehovah God and began worshipping other gods. They had started worshipping Moloch by offering up their children as sacrifices. They had grown weary of waiting on Jehovah God so, they had stopped depending on the God of Heaven because of their frustration and fatigue. They had left their principles and entered into their own perversion. Because of the state of God's, chosen people, God raised up Jeremiah.

* * * * * *

God raised up Jeremiah for the purpose of "crying loud and sparing not." Many have labeled Jeremiah as the "weeping prophet" because Jeremiah was different from the other prophets of his time. Jeremiah did not have a glorious ministry because he was always bringing correction, clarity, and consecration to the people of God. As a matter of fact, the

Bible also states that that Jeremiah was even commissioned to a region or areas that others even refused to go. Prophets are influencers because they are often called into places in which others refused to go.

Judah was considered the group who God commissioned to usher the nation into praise. Here is the question: How can praisers become perverted? Influencer, if you're not careful, you'll only go through the motions and all of the religious movements, but your heart will become distant and far from God. You'll have a *"form of godliness, but you will deny the very power thereof"* (2 Timothy 3:5) . Influencer, whatever you do, don't allow your praise to become perverted.

* * * * * *

The Influencer's Authenticity

Influencer, God is waiting for your organic praise. You may not believe it but all of the hell and the drama you've been through has created a certain sound that must come forth from only you − a sound that Heaven identifies with and when you refuse to release it, you've entered into perversion. The Prophet Jeremiah was assigned to religious people. These people were considered religious because they turned away from their true identities and when you walk away from your organic, authentic, identity, you now operate in **identity theft**. Did you know that the identity protection business is now a billion dollar industry?

Imagine that: a billion dollar industry comprised of businesses to help you protect what's precious; your identity.

Guess what? Identity theft has now entered the kingdom. Instead of walking in an authentic grace, many have disrespected their own grace and have attempted to walk in another man's grace. However, any time you attempt to walk in another man's grace, it's likely you'll encounter the same warfare that that man has had to endure. But now is not the time to walk away from your identity. No one knows you currently. You may be anonymous and God is about to reveal to your enemy who you are.

Paul said it best in *Romans 8:18* which says, *For I reckon that the sufferings of this present time are not worthy to be compared with the glory which shall be revealed in us.* He's talking about the anonymous glory. You have been asking God to put something there, yet God is saying it is already there, it's just anonymous and now God's getting ready to reveal what's been concealed. Right now influencer, you may be anonymous. No one may be aware of your talent, your grace, or your genius. **Say this: It won't be long now!**

So, *God created man in his own image, in the image of God created he him male and female created he them (Genesis 1:27).* 2 Corinthians 5:17 says, *therefore a man be in Christ, he's a new creature. Old things are passed away, and behold, all things are become new.*

1 Peter 2:9 also says, But you are a chosen generation, a royal priesthood, a holy nation, a peculiar people that you should show forth the praises of him who called you out of darkness into this marvelous light. Then *Galatians 2:20 says, I am crucified with Christ. Nevertheless, I live, not I, but the Christ that now liveth in me and the life that I now live in the flesh I live by the faith of the son of God who love me and gave himself for me. Ephesians 2:10 says, For we are his workmanship, created in Christ Jesus unto good works, which God hath before ordained that we should walk in them.* We see identity in all of the scriptures listed above. Let's hone in on Ephesians 2:10.

As an example and for a moment, let's consider that I'm an inventor and I created the cell phone. It is my invention, I have invented it and I have solely engineered it. This means that because I have made it, that makes me the author of this particular creation. When I engineered and created this phone, I created it to work. Now, because the phone performed so well, I moved on and created the IPAD. I have also engineered all of the parts on the inside of the phone to work in accordance with each other which makes the phone itself operate in its own synchronicity.

So, going back to Ephesians 2:10, in other words, everything that God created works. Influencer, all of your gifts, all of your temperaments, every ounce of your anointing, all of your genius, all of your greatness, all of your talents and abilities, your vision and your calling – they all work! Everything inside of you works!

Your identity was created in Christ, it is centered in Christ, and it is contained in Christ. Identity is the distinguishing of character or personality of an individual. Personality is the combination of characteristics and of the quality of an individual – a distinctive character. So, my identity is not what I say, but it's who I was created to be. Your identity has been created in Christ, not your DNA (genetics).

* * * * * * *

The Characteristics of An Influencer

1. Christ-Centered. When you are Christ centered, you are level-headed and you'll never get confused about who's carrying you and who the honor and glory belongs to.

2. Consecrated. Consecration doesn't mean that you fast or you're praying all the time, but consecration means that you have been called out and you've been separated for a certain assignment(s). Because of your assignment you are aware of your source – which is the altar.

3. Clear in Assignment. When you're clear about your assignment and not vacillating about your purpose, then you're not jealous of other men's assignment(s). You're more inclined to "stay in your lane and flow in your vein." When individuals are double-minded, one day they are this and the next day they are something else, they are more prone to mental torment of bipolar and schizophrenia diseases. God's been waiting on you to get clear, which is why He couldn't give you everything He wanted to give you. He understood that your attention was divided. *A house divided, cannot stand (Mark 3:25). A double-minded man is unstable in all his ways (James 1:8).* Therefore God will take His time while He waits on you to become clear on your assignment(s) and your purpose. God has all of eternity to wait.

4. Consistent. Consistency is the definitive bedrock of an influencer. When you are an influencer, you must be reliable. Your routines must be trackable. Jesus had the same routine. That's how the two men on Emmaus Road knew He was Jesus the Christ. He was consistent in how he blessed the food at that time. He blessed it, broke it and then He gave it. Every time Jesus performed miracles, He always went to a mountain; an elevated place to pray. The Bible says, *he that is holy, let him be holy still (Revelation 22:11).* **Consistency builds credibility.**

5. Cultured. Influencers are cultured and they value diversity. Cultured means possessing the ability to move in and out of certain places, environments and people of whom you are both familiar and unfamiliar with. Influencer, it's now time to cross-pollinate just as bees do when carrying pollen from flower to flower. It's time to learn a new culture, try out a new cuisine, a new experience, make a new friend in another income bracket, and/or travel to another country. Your next assignment(s) may come through the intention of your cross-pollination.

Say this: The bees are coming!

Chapter 4
THE INFLUENCER'S ATMOSPHERE:
Apostolic Environments

When you are in the right atmosphere, you don't have to worry about the seed because the right atmosphere and the environment is conducive for seed to break open and come forth. Could it be that you were under the wrong atmosphere and that's why everything inside of you was dormant? Perhaps this is the reason that everything inside of you was held up? Influencer, you've had this ever since you were in your mother's belly but God had to wait for you to get into the right temperature, the right environment, and the right atmosphere. **You must watch and guard your atmosphere.**

In the spring season, conditions are more favorable for plants and flowers to grow. The days are longer than most days; which means that there is more sunlight and the grass and the flowers seem to spring up from the wet ground overnight. One thing that's interesting about the spring, when there's a good rain and enough water and sunlight, that has occurred overnight, you will look at the plush lawn of grass that you previously mowed and wonder how did it grow back just that quickly? Guess what? Things in your life are getting ready to 'pop up' overnight. Though you're going through the process, you're in a season now where the process may not take as long as before. **Say this: My process is speeding up!**

But that doesn't happen everywhere. It happens in a certain environment. You might be in a region full of racism, perversion, and religion but if you are connected to an apostolic atmosphere and apostolic influencers, everyone may be impacted but you. That place is called Goshen. Genesis 45:9-10 describes the *Land of Goshen* as the place in Egypt given to the Hebrews by Pharaoh. During this time, Israel and Egypt were susceptible to the plagues that had been released upon the land but God's people found a place in the middle of all of the destruction and it was called Goshen. They were protected and preserved right there in Goshen, in the midst of all of the chaos. **Say this: I'm apart of the remnant of God.**

* * * * * *

Types of Favorable Environments

In order to grow and develop properly, you must protect your atmosphere. Growth occurs in favorable conditions. You and I grow effectively when we are surrounded by people and opportunities who are conducive to our development. There are several types of favorable atmospheres.

43

Prophetic Atmosphere. *1 Samuel 10:6 says, and the spirit of the Lord will come upon thee and thou shalt prophesied with them, and that in turn be turned into another man.* Prophetic atmospheres happen when the word of the Lord is released with power and instruction. Influencer, **you must** be in an atmosphere where the word of the Lord is released with power and instruction. The word of God comes with demonstration, power, impact and transformation. In a prophetic atmosphere, everything in your life must come subject.

The Bible confirms that Saul was not a prophet, but he was a king. However, because he entered into the prophetic atmosphere, he began to prophesy. Influencer, in a prophetic atmosphere, you should prophesy occasionally. The prophetic atmosphere is accompanied by demonstration and power and it should transform and shift you out of your comfort zone.

Protected Atmosphere. *Matthew 21:12-13 says, and Jesus went into the temple of God, and cast out all them that sold and bought in the temple, and overthrew the tables of the moneychangers, and the seats of them that sold doves, And said unto them, It is written, My house shall be called the house of prayer; but ye have made it a den of thieves.* Here we must protect and preserve the space where God dwells in order to continue to receive the words that God wants to perform. We must be very careful regarding the space that God uses. Kathryn Kuhlman was quoted saying that she would come to the temple of the church every single day at a certain time to pray. She said after a few years, God Himself began to open the doors for her upon entry – because she protected and preserved the space that was meant for God to occupy.

Promised Atmosphere. When the word of the Lord has already been established in a place before the work materializes. *Mark 5:40 says, And they laughed him to scorn. But when he had put them all out, he taketh the father and the mother of the damsel, and them that were with him, and entereth in where the damsel was lying.* Now this is Jairus' daughter who was already dead. First she was ill, but then there was an interruption that prolonged the trip and she died. When Jesus finally arrives and everyone is now mocking, laughing and asking Jesus, "why are you here? Why trouble the master when she's already deceased?In other words, there was an extreme amount of doubt in this atmosphere. However, Jesus' response was, "don't worry, she will arise." In other words, the promise was present before the person arrived.

The promise will always proceed the person the when the Word of the Lord has already been established in a place.

Powerful Atmosphere. An atmosphere infused with the power of God that causes signs, wonders and miracles. *Acts 2:1-4 (KJV), And when the day of Pentecost was fully come, they were all with one accord in one place. And suddenly there* *came a sound from heaven as of a rushing mighty wind, and it filled all the house where they were sitting. And there appeared unto them cloven tongues like as of fire, and it sat upon each of them. And they were all filled with the Holy Ghost, and began to speak with other tongues, as the Spirit gave them utterance.*

Chapter 5
BAD INFLUENCERS

As we continue to look at various individuals that are considered influencers in our society, we understand that if they even touch a product or endorse a service, that product or service will sell out. So many authors became millionaires overnight because Oprah endorsed their stories. Oprah and other celebrities are considered contemporary influencers, but there are also biblical influencers. In 1 Samuel the first chapter, Hannah is depicted as a **prayerful influencer**. The Book of Esther depicts Esther as a **prominent influencer.** In John 4, the woman at the well was a **progressive influencer**. This woman had five husbands and the man she was currently with wasn't hers. So when she came in contact with Jesus, after she gave Him water He essentially said that He was going to put something in her belly that would cause her to never thirst for Jacob's well again. **Say this: God's about to quench my thirst!**

* * * * * *

Then there's David who was considered a **passionate influencer**. The Bible says that when the glory was coming back to Israel, David was dancing. He was dancing so hard that his ephod had fallen off. An ephod is a sleeveless garment usually worn by priests.

The prophet Elijah was a **prophetic influencer**. Just exactly how was Elijah a prophetic influencer? Elijah confronted Jezebel, who at the time was hunting and killing the prophets of God and in the process she was attempting to erase and replace these prophets with her own false prophets of Baal. Elijah challenged the entire system instituted by the Jezebelic agenda on Mount. Carmel by commanding her prophets to call down fire from Heaven. When they attempted to do so, nothing happened. However, when Elijah and God's true prophets began to open their mouths and call on the God of Israel, then instantly fire fell from Heaven.

But this act alone wasn't the influence. The influence was when Ahab (Jezebel's husband), the one that cursed Jehovah and said He didn't exist was now the one who inevitably said he wanted everyone to bow their knee to the God of Elijah. Ahab was the king at the time and because of his authority (Elijah's influence) his decree was law.

Other influencer types: political influencers, prayerful influencers, prominent influencers, progressive influencers, passionate influencers, and prophetic influencers. With any good story, we can't have protagonists without antagonists. Let's take a look at a few antagonists of influencers – **bad influencers.**

Revelations 12:7 says, and a war broke out in heaven. Michael and his angels fought with the Dragon and the dragon and his angels fought, but they did not prevail, nor was a place found to them in heaven any longer. Satan is a bad influencer. The Bible tells us that a war broke out in heaven because satan, Lucifer, the son of the morning, wanted to be God. He wanted to be God because he got tired of walking in his own assignment.

* * * * * *

Satan thought his assignment was seasonal. However, influencer, it is important for you to understand that your assignment is actually a life-long journey. Over the course of your life, your assignment doesn't change, it should grow and it should evolve. You may start out as an intercessor, but you'll grow into a national prophet. You may start out as a prophet, but now you are a political figure. Your assignment doesn't change, but in the right environment and with the right development it should grow and it should evolve. **Say this: I am gaining weight because I am growing, I am developing, and I am evolving.**

49

It's also important to know that when you deny, rebel, refuse to accept or embrace your divine assignment, then warfare will occur.

1. Satan is a bad influencer. Because he wanted to be God, he convinced one-third of heaven to follow him and God kicked them all out of heaven. Satan got tired of his own assignment and he started comparing and competing himself against Jehovah. When you get frustrated with your current assignment, then you will be tempted to compare and compete with others. You must be intentional about "staying in your lane and flowing in your vein" - in other words, work your own assignment.

Genesis 3:1 says, Now the serpent was more subtle than any beast of the field which the Lord God had made. And he said unto the woman, Yea, hath God said, Ye shall not eat of every tree of the garden? The serpent here was a bad influencer. The serpent was more subtle than any beast of the field. That means he was more crafty and cunning. Have you ever had a great movie date, but you sat by the wrong person? Have you ever had a great morning? You had a good breakfast, you ate your *Wheaties* , you felt good, but you went into work and somebody said something that literally a messed your spirit up? Have you ever had a good morning but you went to school and made a mistake and sat by someone that had a negative attitude and their negative attitude affected you? **That's a serpent.**

2. Serpents are bad influencers. Notice that the serpent slithers on its belly. The belly is actually considered the seat of your appetite. Be careful who you allow to talk to you when they speak out of the belly of their appetite; which is their emotions. Now a serpent is another word for snake and a snake has interesting features. One distinguishing feature is that they have a split tongue. When "snakes or serpents" are with you, they speak well of you. But when they are outside of your presence, they will sabotage your name.

A snake can also camouflage itself in certain environments. They can change colors or even seem to transform textures. Some people are one way with you and when you catch them outside of their habitat, they act as if they don't even know who you are.

Numbers 26:10 says the earth opened up and the earth opened her mouth and swallowed them up together with Korah when the company died. Strife is also a bad influencer. Strife is anger and bitter sometimes violent conflict or dissension; disagreement. But it's a disagreement over fundamental issues when people try to move you from or remove your pillars. A pillar is a core value and belief you have for yourself for your family. For example, my pillars are my faith, my family and my future. You cannot tell me that Jesus is NOT the son of God.

3. Strife is a bad influencer. Strife is when people would try to divide or tear you from what you ascribe to. For instance, you're not a drinker but people will try to make you drink or make you feel a negative way if you don't. You're not a smoker but people will try to make you smoke or make you feel a negative way if you don't. You must be intentional about avoiding strife because strife comes with anger. When anger is finished with you, you become bitter. When bitterness is finished with you, here comes rage. The extreme manifestation is murder. One strategy for combating strife is through forgiveness. You must be intentional about the process of forgiveness of those that have hurt you, offended you, rejected you, hurt you or disappointed you. Forgiveness is important to your perspective and how you view the world, your nation, your ministry, leaders and even relationships.

4. Sin is also a bad influencer. *Galatians 5:9 declares that a little leaven leaveneth the whole lump.* Some people may not have core values or beliefs and they say "yes" to every door and opportunity. There are no standards in place because there are no pillars. How much money does it take for you to sell your soul? This is the question on the floor. Even a little sin can disrupt an entire process. Money is a great tool. As an influencer it is a very necessary resource to make things happen and to get things done. But if you're not careful, money can mess you up and cause you to forget about your core values, beliefs, and your pillars while you are chasing resources; money. *1 Timothy 6:10 says, For the love of money is the root of all evil: which while some coveted after, they have erred from the faith, and pierced themselves through with many sorrows.* This scripture is clear; it is not money that is the root of all evil, but it is the love of it; the greed and the coveting of it. It is the little leaven that leaveneth the whole lump.

So bad influencers are: satan, serpent, strife and sin. You are an influencer. This means, that when you step into the room, the assignment of your enemy shifts. Why? 1) You have been appointed which means that your life and who you are has been predestined. 2) You have been approved. This means that God is going to partner with you. *Romans 8:29-30 says, For those God foreknew he also predestined to be conformed to the image of his Son, that he might be the firstborn among many brothers and sisters. And those he predestined, he also called; those he called, he also justified; those he justified, he also glorified.* Therefore you were chosen, appointed and approved by God before the foundations of the world. You didn't come from your mother and you didn't come from your father, you came through them. When God said in Genesis, "let there be light," – you were right there.

I have written this manual to destroy every satanic plot of the enemy for emerging influencers that would have you to think that because you look like your mother and you sound like your father, you are limited to their generational curses and their generational cycles. But according to Galatians, Jesus took the curse and because Jesus took the curse we can be influencers and walk into God's blessings and destiny for our lives. **Say this: I've been appointed by God to move in my metron!**

As discussed previously, your metron is your sphere, your territory and your rule. Your metron is also your assignment(s) and sphere where your grace will operate without being hindered. I sometimes like to use examples to demonstrate this by identifying the metron of practical things, i.e the metron of a bird: the sky. The metron of a fish: water. The metron of a football player: the field. The metron of a basketball player: the court. When you're moving in your metron your gift will work unhindered.

Therefore, when you step in the bank or the meeting, when you step in the boardroom or when you step into this large room that God's about to prepare for you, I want to encourage you not to be intimidated. However, I must warn you that you're going to feel insecure. You may even feel a little insufficient, but I want you to understand that you are already predestined. You have been appointed to walk in this level.

Say this: I BELONG HERE because I am an influencer!

Matthew 28:20 says, *teaching them to observe all things whatsoever I have commanded you: and, lo, I am with you always, even unto the end of the world.* God is about to get in the boat of your assignment and link arms with you so you'll know that even in the times that you might feel that you can't make it, He's going to pull the load for you! Therefore, He's already approved you! He's already a partner with you. Imagine that? Jehovah is your partner!

Not only has God appointed you and approved you, but He's also anointed you. *Matthew 10:1* says, *and when he had called into his 12 disciples, he gave them power.* After the call comes the commission. *And when he had called unto him his 12 disciples, he gave them power (Matthew 10:1).* God will never give you purpose without power. Because if He gives you a purpose without power, then He's setting you up for suicide because you will never be able to do what He's called you to do in your own natural ability. You will never be able to do what He's called you to do in your own natural strength.

Therefore, God has not only 1) approved and 2) appointed you, but He has also 3) accelerated you. *Ephesians 5:16 says, Redeeming the time because the days are evil.* God is now redeeming the times which means that God's shortening up the days so that you'll get to your assignment quicker. Previously, the things that took you months to accomplish is now only going to take you weeks and the things that took you weeks to execute and finish will now only take you days. You're going to be able to accomplish this through inspiration, information, and ignition.

* * * * * *

Inspiration is powerful because when inspiration came upon Nehemiah, he began to inspire the Jews who had already been dejected. Nehemiah inspired an entire group of people to follow him back to Israel and then he gave them a new assignment which was to rebuild the broken down walls. Come follow me back to Israel. It takes inspiration and return to the place of failure and believe God for the fantastic.

Because you are a solutionist, problem-solver, and a power source, get ready influencer, you're now moving into your finest hour. You've been small. You've been obscure. You've had opposition and opposition is only an indicator that the outstanding is on its way!

Say this: I am on the right path and I am ready to receive God's outstanding!

Chapter 6
FEAR & FRUSTRATION:
Hindrances of an Influencer

Influencer, right now, you may be frustrated with ministry, your mission or you may even be frustrated with man. It can happen and it does happen. During my time of releasing this *influencer* revelation, I asked how many influencers were dealing with the **spirit of frustration**. Almost the entire room raised their hand and confessed that they were currently dealing with frustration in some way, shape or form. *Frustration* is the plight of the influencer, the mover and the shaker, and the world-changer. Frustration is one of the biggest hindrances Satan uses to 1) discourage, 2) distract and even 3) divide the influencer from their dominant assignment(s).

Everyone has multiple assignments and unfortunately what has been happening is that you've been dealing with your minor assignments, but you have not tapped into your major assignments. Frustration causes discouragement and the enemy wants to divide and distract the influencer from their dominant assignment. Frustration is the feeling of being upset and annoyed; especially because of the inability to change or achieve something. Frustration is a strong emotion and it is normally fostered because there is the feeling of lacking the ability to change or achieve something.

Frustration is fostered when the individual feels the pressure of the inability, but not when others are not doing or achieving. Aspiration, annoyance, anger, vexation, irritation; frustration fosters a flawed foundation of faith. When you are frustrated:

1) You compromise the principles of God. Because when you're frustrated, you may say, I'm going to take the easy way out. Did God really say that? Did God really mean that for me?

2) You cancel the process of God. God has a process and He has a system for instituting a new movement. *Mark 4:28 says, For the earth bringeth forth fruit of herself; first the blade, then the ear, after that the full corn in the ear.* He said, **first** the blade, **then** the ear. God will never take you from the ear to the full ear. *In Exodus 23:30,* He says, *By little and little I will drive them out from before thee, until thou be increased, and inherit the land.* We go from faith to faith. Meaning, that God deals in process. He builds in levels. For instance, my oldest daughter graduated from one of the top 10 schools for women in the country. Though she has always been intelligent, when she entered collegiate-level education, she had to start her process all over again: freshmen, sophomore, junior and then senior before she earned her collegiate level degree. There was still a process she had to go through – though she had already mastered a previous process at another level (high school). I know you may think that you are well-advanced and you don't need a process, but you need the process because every level is working something pertinent in you and for your assignment(s) **Say this: Everything I had to endure was working together for the good.**

3) Cages the potential of God. It is hard for God to perform the fantastic in the lives of his people because most times they don't believe Him. In one demonstration, I grabbed a team of men and had them surround me while I tried to break out of the barrier I'd asked them create. This is how God has been restricted and blocked from moving in the lives of some influencers. No faith or low faith restricts the movement of God. Imagine that: An almighty, all-powerful, all-knowing, and all present God can be blocked or restricted? The answer is – yes. He is a **sovereign** God.

Sovereign means that although God has supreme and ultimate power, sovereign in this sense is also defined as one that exercises supreme authority *within a limited sphere*. Therefore, God submits Himself under the rule that He has instituted and He can go no farther. He can go no farther than your frustration.

So what we thought was faith was really fear.

Anytime fear is present, faith is absent. Anytime you are afraid, you are afraid of the uncertainty, you are afraid of the unknown – faith is absent. What if I do that? What's going to happen if I step this way? What's going to happen if I do what God has called me to do, what's going to happen if I step out with my company? What's going to happen? I don't have enough capital to start this company. I need more money to start this ministry. But if Noah would have waited until the first day he saw rain, it would have been too late and it would have been too late for him to execute the building of the ark as God had commissioned him. Therefore influencer, I give you permission. Starting tomorrow, start it. Even if you have to start in your basement, start it. You may have to begin in your living room, but start it. As a matter of fact, your living room may be your studio or your office – but **START IT!**

For we walk by faith and not by sight (2 Corinthians 5:7). We walk by divine revelation, not physical appearance. So what we thought was faith was really fear and for some, this has been the hindrance and this is how you have been operating. You think you are moving in faith; however because of fear, your hands are tied behind your back and you have *limited* (if any) mobility. When you think you're moving in faith, you are moving, but you are not obtaining and you can't obtain when your arms are tied behind your back. Listen, you've got vision, you've got dreams, and you've got potential. But evidently, you're lacking the ability to obtain. That's all right influencer, we decree that the

the spirits of fear and frustration are going to break off of your life! *2 Timothy 1:7 says, For God hath not given us the spirit of fear; but of power, and of love, and of a sound mind.*

* * * * * *

Frustration enters in because you have been trying to place new content into your current context. *Mark 2: 22 says, And no man putteth new wine into old bottles: else the new wine doth burst the bottles, and the wine is spilled, and the bottles will be marred: but new wine must be put into new bottles.*

Jesus says this: no one – not a prophet, not a priest, not a preacher; no one puts new wine in an old bottle because if you put new wine in an old bottle – the bottle, the container, or the structure, will be damaged or otherwise destroyed. So Jesus instituted an order that if I acquire new substance, it must be placed into an entirely new structure. You must put new content in a whole new context.

Influencer, you have been receiving fresh revelation and THAT'S been your frustration. You've received new content but you are attempting to place it in your current context.

Chapter 7
CONTENT & CONTEXT

Context is the setting in which a phrase or a word is used. However, content are the words or the ideas that make up a piece that holds it together. **Content** is what we are talking about. Context is how we're talking about it. Content is what you write. Context is the meaning behind what you write. For example, content says: there is no God, but then context is the "fool says in his own heart. There is no God (Psalm 14:1)."

An analogy would be a container and the container is the context. What's in the container is the content. So any good narrative contains the who, what, when, where, why, and the how. So, the who, when, where is the setting – which is the context. The what, why and how action of the scenes is the content. For example: My name is Travis Jennings. My mother is Felicia. My father is Andre. I grew up with my great grandmother in East Lake Meadows on Daniels Street. I've revealed a lot of context. Going a little further: I was raised in severe poverty and I grew up with feelings of rejection and abandonment. I was told every single day that I would be nothing and nobody. Now, I've also revealed content. **Content is the substance. Context is the structure**.

In Mark 2: 22 Jesus says I've got to put something new in you. Now that you have it, I have to place you into something new because you've been trying to put this new content into your current context and that's why you have been frustrated. That is why you have been aggravated. That's why you have been vexed in your spirit because you have been receiving the revelation that you are a reformer. You have been receiving revelation, that you are a ministry mogul. You have been receiving revelation, that you are an influencer. You have been receiving revelation about your metron. You have been receiving all of this revelation and looking at your current context that seems to be inconsistent. You have received revelation about who you are and where you are going and it is just not adding up.

So what happens when what is on the inside of you does not resemble your current? **You're going through frustration.** But don't worry, you are building context and adding content. That is why you are placing yourself in the wrong context because you have become familiar with your current size.

You have been familiar with this particular size ever since you came out of your mother's womb and you've still got baby booties on your feet. You're now cramming new content into an old context and you're also dumbing yourself down so that the people around you don't feel stupid or intimidated. You're cramming new context into the old content that other people have created for you. That's why you don't want to let them go and leave them because you are afraid of the new context. However, if you let the old go, it will make room for the new. You need content right now and God will always give content before he gives context.

Let's look at Moses: Moses, you are NOT Pharaoh's son. But, you ARE a deliverer and you're going to be raised up to bring the Israelites out of Egypt (content); however, Moses still found himself back in the old context. How about David? Currently, you're in the sheep field, but you are a man after God's own heart. You are the prophetic psalmist of Israel (content), but he went right back to his old context – which was herding the sheep even after the prophet revealed this to him. David was anointed king (content), but he did not take the throne right away (context). Then there was Gideon who was the weakest of his family; even his whole tribe, but you're are a mighty man of valor. You're going to deliver the children of Israel out of the hand of the Midianites. However, after this revelation, Gideon went right back to the winepress.

Here is Esther's content: Though you're going to be the queen, it looks as though there is nothing to you. Why? Because God never gives you new context without first giving you new content. So Esther's new content is that she is the queen of Israel. God's going to raise her up and she's going to marry the king. Esther's new content is that she is the one God is going to raise up to spare his people.

You have insight with the right content. *John 16:6-7 says, But because I have said these things unto you, sorrow hath filled your heart, Nevertheless I tell you the truth (content); It is expedient for you that I go away: for if I go not away, the Comforter will not come unto you; but if I depart, I will send him unto you.*

In this scripture, Jesus declares that it is expedient for you; it's advantageous for you and to your advantage that I go away. Jesus says, I've already given you new content. I am the content; I am the revelation, but I can't place all that I am in you in this form so it is expedient that I go away. However, when I go away, another context will transpire for you!

Get ready influencer! Things are about to change for you and one of the first things that's going to happen is that your container is going to change!

Chapter 8
PROPHETIC INFLUENCE

We've previously discussed different influencer types: prominent influencers (Esther), progressive influencers (the woman at the well), passionate influencer (David) and even political influencers (Nehemiah). We've looked at both secular influencers and sacred (biblical) influencers. We've even discussed some hindrances and plights of influencers. In this chapter, we're going to address prophetic influencers.

Let's not lose sight of you as the influencer. The reason you have that career, that job or that business and the reason you're making moves in that industry, and the reason why God sent you into the Body of Christ is because because you're getting **ready to make an aposotolic shift!** You are an influencer!

Say this: I AM an influencer!

* * * * * *

The Purpose of the Prophetic.

The purpose of the prophetic is to infuse one and cause them to be awakened to what they've been called and commissioned to do ultimately catapulting them into destiny.

The Potential of the Prophetic.

The potential of the prophetic is to invite one to a reality that was once off limits. It is to open possibilities that were once closed.

The Progression of the Prophetic.

The progression of the prophetic is to cause the believer to be infused with supernatural momentum that causes the moment to accelerate.

The Protection of the Prophetic.

In Psalms 5:12 David said, "Surely, LORD, you bless the righteous; you surround them with your favor as with a shield. With Elijah, The Lord sent a chariot (which are used for war) and not only did he send a chariot but it was on fire. It's important to note that historically, chariots were often used for war. That's the protection of the prophetic. God didn't want anyone to interrupt the ascension of Elijah.

The Promise of the Prophetic

The promise of the prophetic is when the believer starts walking into the prophetic manifestation based on the prophetic word that was spoken over their lives.

In 1 Samuel 10:6-12, the Prophet Samuel is in the middle of releasing the word of the Lord to King Saul. He declares, And the Spirit of the Lord will come upon thee, and thou shalt prophesy with them, and shalt be turned into another man.7 And let it be, when these signs are come unto thee, that thou do as occasion serve thee; for God is with thee.6. **And** the Spirit of the Lord will come upon thee, and thou shalt prophesy with them, and shalt be turned into another man.

In Samuel the 10th chapter, we see that Saul the Benjamite has been anointed to be the King of Israel by Samuel the prophet. Saul was previously on a journey to recover runaway goats from his father's flock and found himself in the presence of the prophet Samuel who was both a seer and judge for Israel in that day. Saul figures since there is a seer nearby I can simply inquire of him concerning the goats, not knowing that God had already prophetically sent Samuel to that location. Samuel gives him the information he wants about the goats but the actual purpose of the encounter was to anoint Saul as the future king of Israel. Note: Anytime you're connected to a strong apostolic and prophetic anointing, it will push you into destiny and it will push you into purpose. After Samuel communed with the prophet, Samuel was then able to release the word of the Lord.

Commune means to communicate, speak, talk, converse, to feel at one with; empathize with, identify with, have a rapport with; to relate to, feel close to – in other words, create intimacy with.

* * * * * *

1. The prophetic places you in the presence of the prophet.

Saul began to prophesy by himself. He was connected to one that was greater than himself. He was connected to a prophet but not only that the scripture goes on further to say he communed with him and he honored the prophetic voice. You see, Saul's next level of purpose and destiny was directly connected to the prophetic voice. Saul couldn't prophesy until it was first legislated and legitimize by the prophet. Saul was not a long ranger spirit. He didn't wake up and say: "I feel like prophesying today!" No, he was pronounced and proclaimed by the prophet first. Here's the question: who pronounced you? Who legislated and legitimize your ministry? Did you submit it to the prophet? Have you communed with the prophet? Have you sought wisdom of the prophet in your life.

Here is another question: do you truly know the significance of the prophetic voice? When was the last time you honored the prophetic voice? When was the last time you obeyed the prophetic voice?

Amos 3:7 (KJV) says, Surely the Lord GOD will do nothing, but he reveals his secret unto his servants the prophets. We can see here that the prophetic is the voice of God and how can you hear the voice of God without the prophet?

Romans 10:13-14 says, For whosoever shall call upon the name of the Lord shall be saved. How then shall they call on him in whom they have not believed? And how shall they believe in him of whom they have not heard? And how shall they hear without a preacher? In other words, there's an order and protocol to the prophetic. What is the prophetic without the prophet? It was when the prophet released the prophetic word of God over Saul's life that he was activated. Being in the presence of the prophet activated the identity of Saul. Never down play being in the presence of the prophet. There are some things regarding your destiny that can only be activated by the prophetic voice. Some endowments require an endorsement!

And so how does the Prophetic Influence people? 1) It places them in the presence of the Prophet!

2) It penetrates your heart preparing you for purpose. In 1 Samuel 10:9, we discover that God gave Saul a new heart! The heart of a man is the focus of his physical and spiritual being. The heart is also known as the seat of **one's intentions.**

Proverbs 4:23 Above all else, guard your heart, for everything you do flows from it.

Proverbs 27:19 As water reflects the face, so one's life reflects the heart.

Jeremiah 17:9 The heart is deceitful above all things and beyond cure. Who can understand it? "I the Lord search the heart!"

God cares about the state of our hearts. He's very concerned about what matters most to us. He cares about the things we care about. He's concerned about our passions and convictions. These things are extremely important to God especially concerning the prophetic. The prophetic is the voice of God and God will always challenge you in your character and in your convictions. So the prophetic will began to cleanse your heart.

Amos 3:3 KJV says, How can two walk together except they be agreed. Well to agree with God means that you not only love Him but that you love what He loves and you hate what He hates. If you say you love God with all your heart, how can you say love God and still do things He hates with absolutely no conviction? How can you say you love God and still drink alcohol? Not only that but how can you say you love God when you have hate in your heart for your brother?

3) It properly postures you into alignment with the company of Prophetic Presbytery.

1 *Samuel 10:10 says, And when they came thither to the hill, behold, a company of prophets met him; and the Spirit of God came upon him, and he prophesied among them.* When Saul's heart changed, he could properly operate in the company that was always meant for him to accompany. Some of us have problems in our social life because we are in the wrong company. We hang around the wrong people. You might ask yourself why do I always find myself around or attract the same type of people? Does it seem like everybody around you are liars? Steal? Or perhaps they are full of drama? Maybe they are living paycheck to paycheck? Petty? I don't know, you might want to check your heart.

When Saul's heart changed his company changed. When his company changed his countenance changed. When his countenance changed his capabilities changed. You see, when Saul found his tribe he began to thrive! 1 Samuel 10 not only gives us Saul's process of how he shifted into the prophetic but it also gives us the order development in the prophetic. Particularly for those who feel that have been called into the prophetic call as it relates to the five fold ministry.

There is an order of development to the prophetic call. First is the pronunciation of the prophetic on your life by the apostle/prophet. Then as you continue to go through the process of transformation you should receive a new heart posture and new passions. Then your character lines up with your call. In the timing of God, when time and chance kiss, when God gives you the green light, He then properly postures you into alignment with prophetic people or a prophetic presbytery.

Again when Saul found his tribe he began to thrive. My question is: who is your tribe? Who do you agree with? Your network will determine your net worth! Whatever you keep looking at you will become. When you consider this text, you see that when Saul got around the company of prophets they didn't come down to his level, he had to ascend to their level. That's call impact. In others words, the prophetic will influence the people in your life to either shape up or to ship out. Yes, the prophetic will always cause you to leave old playmates and old playgrounds alone.

Chapter 9
POWER TO PROPHESY & PERPETUAL PROMOTION

From our previous chapter, we have learned a few things about the prophetic as it relates to influencers. The prophetic 1) **places you in the presence of the prophet; 2) it penetrates your heart, preparing you for purpose; and then 3) it properly postures you into alignment in the company of prophetic presbytery.**

There is an order, protocol and process for walking in the prophetic as in influencer. In keeping with our text in 1 Samuel, if we go back a chapter to 1 Samuel 9, we learn that initially, Saul had low self-esteem. He was the tallest man around but he still thought very low of himself. That all changed. The prophetic will cause you to have confidence in the areas where you once were unsure. And Saul answered and said, Am not I a Benjamite, of the smallest of the tribes of Israel? and my family the least of all the families of the tribe of Benjamin? wherefore then speakest thou so to me?

4. The prophetic PROPELS YOU WITH POWER TO PROPHESY.

In chapter 9, Saul was scared. He was a chump. But in chapter 10 he'd started prophesying and was transformed into a champ. People had even began to question and doubt his transformation as we can see in verse 11 when they'd started asking is Saul now one of the prophets? Say this: I'm now shifting from a chump into a champ!

5. The prophetic PRODUCES PERPETUAL PROMOTION.

I Samuel 13 says, And when he had made an end of prophesying, he came to the high place. So the prophetic shifted Saul from a chump to a champ Champ; from feeling like the least of his tribe, to prophesying in the high place – to the King of Israel. This is an example of **perpetual promotion**. Influencer, you are going to win. When you win this time, you're going to win again!

Extra - extra, get ready to read all about it! The enemy had you looking down on yourself. Looking down on your family, looking down on your capabilities. You were stuck chasing goats around, menial tasks had you stuck in a rut. But influencer, it's time to prophesy! It's time to change your environment and your circumstances. Influencer – prophesy!

INFLUENCER DECLARATIONS

I **decree and declare** that I will access and obtain the purpose of the prophetic, the potential of the prophetic promise and the progression of the prophetic in Jesus name!

I **decree and declare** that the prophetic places me in the presence of the prophet!

I **decree and declare** that the prophetic penetrates my heart preparing me for purpose!

I **decree and declare** that the prophetic properly postures me in alignment with prophetic Presbytery!

I **decree and declare** that the prophetic propels me with power to prophesy and I **decree and declare** that the prophetic produces perpetual promotion in my life, in Jesus name!!

Chapter 10
RULING FROM TWO DIMENSIONS

Many around the world have already grabbed onto this revelation of the influencer and have begun to move with the prophetic release and apostolic thrust. As influencers, we are also supposed to rule from more than one dimension. Not only are we supposed to have favor, but we are supposed to have flavor – just as salt has flavor. As intercessors, we should have influence in heaven and on earth.

Matthew 5:13-16 says, first that you are the salt of the earth and then it says that you are the light of the world. Earth here means region, land, country, and ground. As we read further He shifts it and says that "you are the light of the world." World in this sense doesn't mean region; the word *world* here means cosmos. Here, Jesus is saying is that **you have influence in two dimensions.**

You have influence in the natural dimension (earth) and you also have influence in the supernatural (the cosmos). The cosmos is where principalities, powers and the rulers of darkness of this world, spiritual wickedness in high places reside (as outlined in Ephesians 6). Therefore, you have authority in your region and you also have authority in the realm of the spirit. When you enter in your region and you may notice that racism and sexism exists there. Because of this, you may find that people may treat you differently because of the color of your skin or you may find that they are treating you differently because of the origin of your sex. Influencer, you are now in that region be salt and to be light – to rule simultaneously in two dimensions. **Say this: The assignment of my enemy has shifted!**

* * * * * *

As an influencer, I want you to understand the power and dominion you possess while you are moving forward in your destiny. As kingdom influencers, we have been given certain access as it relates to prayer and intercession so we can be effective here on earth.

I. Prophetic Intercession: When you say something in the spirit that affects the natural, like closing the heavens. I Kings 17 says, *And Elijah the Tishbite, of the inhabitants of Gilead, said to Ahab, "As the Lord God of Israel lives, before whom I stand, there shall not be dew nor rain these years,* *except at my word. Then the word of the Lord came to him, saying, get away from here and turn eastward, and hide by the Brook Cherith, which flows into the Jordan. And it will be that you shall drink from the brook, and I have commanded the ravens to feed you there. So he went and did according to the word of the Lord, for he went and stayed by the Brook Cherith, which flows into the Jordan.* The ravens brought him bread and meat in the morning, and bread and meat in the evening; and he drank from the brook. And it happened after a while that the brook dried up, because there had been no rain in the land.

In other words, you have been given the power to dry up and destroy every antagonizing spirit and it will no longer affect you.

I Kings 18:41- 46 talks about opening the heavens. If you have power to close, you have power to open. *Then Elijah said to Ahab, Go up, eat and drink; for there is the sound of abundance of rain. So Ahab went up to eat and drink. And Elijah went up to the top of Carmel; then he bowed down on the ground, and put his face between his knees, and said to his servant, go up now, look toward the sea. So he went up and looked, and said, there is nothing. And seven times he said, Go again. Then it came to pass the seventh time, that he said, "There is a cloud, as small as a man's hand, rising out of the sea!" So he said, "Go up, say to Ahab, Prepare your chariot, and go down before the rain stops you. Now it happened in the meantime that the sky became black with clouds and wind, and there was a heavy rain. So Ahab rode away and went to Jezreel. Then the hand of the Lord came upon Elijah; and he* *girded up his loins and ran ahead of Ahab to the entrance of Jezreel.*

* * * * * *

2) Physical intercession (known as travailing intercession). When you will feel the pain in the physical in order bring about release in the spiritual. *Luke 22:39-46, Coming out, Jesus went to the Mount of Olives, as He was accustomed, and His disciples also followed Him. When He came to the place, He said to them, "Pray that you may not enter into temptation." And He was withdrawn from them about a stone's throw, and He knelt down and prayed, saying, "Father, if it is Your will, take this cup away from Me; nevertheless not My will, but Yours, be done." Then an angel appeared to Him from heaven, strengthening Him. And being in agony, He prayed more earnestly. Then His sweat became like great drops of blood falling down to the ground. When He rose up from prayer, and had come to His disciples, He found them sleeping from sorrow. Then He said to them, "Why do you sleep? Rise and pray, lest you enter into temptation.*

Hebrews 12: 2 says, looking unto Jesus, the author and finisher of our faith, who for the joy that was set before Him endured the cross, despising the shame, and has sat down at the right hand of the throne of God.

You can't effectively travail with heavy weights and sin in your life. Think about this: when a woman goes into labor, she's so sensitive and the smallest of things can irritate her. When she's preparing to have her baby, she doesn't want anything touching her because the physical pain causes her emotions to run wild. Spiritual travailing is similar to natural labor because physical pain from the act can cause your emotions to run wild; which can cause your faith to be in conflict with your flesh.

3) Petitioning Intercession. When you have to perform an act in the both the natural and spiritual in order to bring about an actual change in the natural through intercession.

A petition is a formal request for something asked in a respectful and humble manner. As influencers, there are matters out of our sphere of authority that we must take before the courtroom of Heaven. *1 John 5:14-15 (AMP), And this is confidence (the assurance, the privilege of boldness) which we have in Him: [we are sure] that if we ask anything (make any request) according to His will (in agreement with His own plan), He listens to and hears us. 15 And if (since) we [positively] know that He listens to us in whatever we ask, we also know [with settled and absolute knowledge] that we have [granted us as our present possessions] the requests made of Him.*

Numbers 27:1-11 also vividly outlines how Moses brought the daughters of Zelophehad's case of their inheritance from their father before the Lord. In those days, property of the deceased automatically went to the son(s) of the family. In this case, there was no son. Zelophehad had all daugthers. So they brought the case to Moses and Moses took it before the Lord in the courtroom of Heaven. The daughters of Zelophehad were

Mahlah, Noah, Hoglah, Milkah and Tirzah. They came forward and stood before Moses, Eleazar the priest, the leaders and the the whole assembly at the entrance to the tent of the meeting and said, *"Our father died in the wilderness. He was not among Korah's followers, who banded together against the LORD, but he died for his own sin and left no sons. Why should our father's name disappear from his clan because he had no son? Give us property among our father's relatives."* So Moses brought their case before the LORD.

There are matters that can only be handled in the authority of Heaven's courtroom. As an influencer, you must be able to discern which matters should be settled there and when they should be released there. Here is something to consider: Heaven can only rule in your favor when you are in the will of God for your life and your destiny.

The influencer not only has power in the earth, but there are also resources and tools working with the influencer in Heaven in order to accomplish their assignment(s) on earth; thereby ruling in two dimensions.

Say this: I have no excuse because Heaven is on my side!

Chapter 11
INFLUENCING THE AIRWAYS

So far, we've discussed several types of influencers and we've discussed how an influencer rules in two dimensions. I would like to explore the idea of ruling in more than one dimension a little deeper. Let's discuss how we influence the airways. Not only does an influencer have authority when influencing the earth, but you have authority when influencing the airways. Influencer, you're about to receive revelation that will allow you to shut the enemy's transmission down!

There exists **satanic transmissions** which are the pathways the enemy uses to execute his agenda into the earth. Similar to the secret *Underground Railroad* passage that Harriet Tubman used to help slaves escape to freedom, but only the enemy uses pathways to bind up the believer and the influencer.

The *Underground Railroad* was invisible or "not in plain sight." Only her collaborators had knowledge of the *Underground Railroad's* exact path. The enemy uses these "invisible" paths in the spirit realm to sabotage, subvert, constrict, hinder, distract or in an attempt to cause the influencer to abort their earthly assignment(s). But if you can shut down the enemy's pathways, you can cancel his intentions and thereby **shut him down.**

In order to succeed in your assignment influencer, you need knowledge, wisdom, and insight concerning these pathways. There are openings in the heavens that grant the enemy access that must be closed.

Transmission is the process of sending digital or analog data (radio waves) over a communication medium (a frequency) to one or more computing, network, communication or electronic devices. It enables the transfer and communication of devices in a point-to-point, point-to-multipoint and multipoint-to-multipoint environment. The enemy has gained entrance, but if you cancel the enemy's pathways, you cancel his agenda.

How the Enemy Gains Entrance – What Passages?

First of all influencer, complete honesty, transparency and vulnerability is key in being able to acknowledge, accept and embrace certain "passages" that grants entry to the enemy. This can be difficult in some but *God not only desires truth in the inward parts, in our innermost being (Psalm 51:6).*

But the Bible also assures us *that the truth will make you free (John 8:32)*. Let's get free and let's get wisdom. Some passages that are demonic gateways to the enemy are:

1) **Generational** – A generational curse is basically a defilement that was passed down from one generation to another. Generational curses are usually involuntary or unintended access points for the enemy. For example, your mother may have dealt with mental diseases of schizophrenia or bipolar disorder and it's likely that this has also been passed down in some form to the children. Maybe a parent was involved in the occult and opened themselves up to other unclean spirits; which may have also been passed along to the children. The Bible tells us that the sin of the parents can cause that same pollution to be handed down to their children: *Lamentations 5:7, "Our fathers have sinned, and are not; and we have borne their iniquities.* There's a passage, a certain transmission that the enemy uses to gain access; which cannot be contended with in the natural.

2) **Sin and Disobedience** – sin is an act of transgression against divine or natural law. Sin can also be viewed as any thought or action that endangers the ideal relationship between an individual and God. This is the most blatant act and deliberate act that creates and direct passage for satanic transmissions. It is this act that originally separated

man from God's presence in Genesis. Being outside of God's presence and provision places us in the clear line of attack of the enemy. God is clear throughout scripture about the effects of sin. Both sin and disobedience are synonymous in the context of satanic transmissions. Disobedience, rebellion, stubbornness is most often a direct result of sin which the Bible denotes as being as the sin of witchcraft in *1Samuel 15:23, For rebellion is as the sin of witchcraft, and stubbornness is as iniquity and idolatry.*

3) **Breaking Covenants** – God is a God of covenant. They are important to God and are the backbone of the storyline of the Bible and the backbone of family. It is quite literally a formal, solemn, or binding agreement. A covenant agreement between God and His people, in which God makes promises to his people and, usually, requires **certain conduct from them.** In the Old Testament, God made agreements with Noah, Abraham, and Moses and the children of Israel. God has also instituted a covenant with us through the sacrifice of Jesus. Covenants are usually accompanied by God's presence, provision, and protection. The enemy hates this so, when covenants are broken (both directly and indirectly), this "hedge" also leaves us prone to the enemy's passages.

If you keep fighting in the natural, you'll miss the wisdom. Let's quickly discuss the wisdom of war.

* * * * * *

The Wisdom of War

Know your enemy

1 Peter 5:8 says, Be sober, be vigilant; because your adversary the devil, as a roaring lion, walketh about, seeking whom he may devour.

James 4:7, Submit yourselves therefore to God. Resist the devil, and he will flee from you

John 10:10, The thief cometh not, but for to steal, and to kill, and to destroy: I am come that they might have life, and that they might have it more abundantly.

2 Corinthians 11:14, And no marvel; for Satan himself is transformed into an angel of light

Influencer, before you engage in war, you must have God's perspective concerning it. This is the **wisdom of war** and there is an order. First, we must *be sober and vigilant* as 1 Peter 5:8 outlines. Then we must submit ourselves and John 10:10 reminds us about whose authority it is we war with. Lastly, 2 Corinthians advises us that our enemy has the capability

87

to "transform." On Monday, he can be one thing and then on Tuesday, your enemy can be something or someone else completely different. This lets us know that we must study our enemy. **Everyone has an enemy.**

Claiming Spiritual Real Estate

In the natural, when you own physical property, you have authority over a particular area. You have paid a price for the land you own and therefore, you can authorize what comes in and what goes out. You have executive and ultimate authority regarding the dealings of that portion of land. When you have spiritual real estate, there is a root in God you have paid for that gives you direct access to God. There is an authority present and a spiritual place that God has given you rulership over – you have the power to open or close and can execute Heaven's plans. You walk in a dimension of kingdom authority in a spiritual area. There is a divine sense of authority and confidence that God hears you and responds. *And this is the confidence that we have in him, that, if we ask any thing according to his will, he heareth us (John 5:14-15).* Here, demons don't just tremble; **they flee** a space, a region or a territory they've been occupying.

Forgiveness

2 Corinthians 2:10-11 says, to whom ye forgive any thing, I forgive also: for if I forgave any thing, to whom I forgave it, for your sakes forgave I it in the person of Christ. Lest Satan should get an advantage of us: for we are not ignorant of his devices. Unforgiveness is device that Satan uses as a passage to gain access and our wisdom of war in this case is forgiveness. Think back over your life – influencer, who do you need to forgive?

For we wrestle not against flesh and blood, but against principalities, against powers, against the rulers of the darkness of this world, against spiritual wickedness in high places, Ephesians 6:12. The word ruler here in the Greek is *cosmocrator* and it means world ruler. We also see it in *2 Corinthians 4:4 which says, whom the god of this world (the cosomocrator) hath blinded the minds of them which believe not, lest the light of the glorious gospel of Christ, who is the image of God, should shine unto them.* World ruling spirits rule over regions and they make fetishes look like fads; witchcraft hide under the guise of "family traditions." These regional spirits make murder look like a life choice and homosexuality look like a lifestyle. These ruling spirits exaggerates reality, causing people to live life by preference instead of on principle.

In a demonstration, I asked seven people to stand up and each represented a specific **Mountain of Influence.** These "spheres" or mountains are the facets of society that must be impacted in order to affect change. These mountains are 1) the church, 2) arts and entertainment, 3) government, 4) family, 5) business, 6) education, and 7) media. I asked our congregation to state who were called to which mountains and mountains and we identified the ruling spirits and principalities associated with their various mountains. We identified:

1) **Church** – Religion. Individuals connected to the sphere of church will always be challenged with remaining in an "old wineskin" and constantly challenged with routine. The spirit of religion may cause individuals that are called to this mountain to remain comfortable instead of reinvention. These individuals are likely to be driven by the "applause of people" instead of the will of God, which will cause them to remain on the same level for 20 years.

2) **Government** – Corruption and Lying. Individuals called to the mountain of government may be enticed by a lying spirit and corruption. These individuals must be intentional about walking in truth and transparency. These individuals love money and power. They love the paper over people.

3) **Family** – Covenant-Breaking. Family is a covenant that starts with a husband and a wife. But family can now extend beyond and are now even blended and comprised of different variations. Individuals called to the mountain of family may be challenged with the spirit of adultery and divorce. These individuals must walk in the spirit of unity and transparency.

4) **Arts and Entertainment** – Lust (Greed), Perversion, Double-Mindedness. These individuals will be challenged with constantly "performing" and having one personality

with one group of people and another personality with others. This mountain is laden with strong perversion and greed so individuals that are called to this mountain must be intentional about guarding themselves from this type of enticement. Biblically speaking, Daniel never defiled himself by eating the king's meat (Daniel 1:8); therefore Influencer, you can be in the presence of great people and not be influenced by their lifestyle.

5) **Business** – Corruption and Idolatry. Individuals called to this mountain may begin to idolize what they produce or what it is they provide, become "intoxicated" and start to believe in their own ability once they become profitable. It's important for entrepreneurs and business owners to be intentional about remaining humble. This may mean volunteering at a local shelter, at your local church and always finding ways to give back.

6) **Education** – Error and Pride. Individuals called to this Mountain of Influence will be prone to thinking they are always right. These individuals often will have the tendency to overthink so these individuals must be intentional about avoiding wrong thinking and overthinking or over analyzing matters.

7) **Media** - Pride, Vanity. Individuals called to this sphere of influence are often responsible for bringing things to life or making things happen. Like artists, these individuals are often very sensitive about what they are produce and seek

credit and validation. They must be intentional about why it is they do what they do and constantly walk in the spirit of humility.

Influencer, if you're going to be a force to reckoned with and influence the airways, you must have wisdom concerning your warfare while you are closing the enemy's passages or satanic transmissions to your assignment. **Say this: I have power, prudence, and the right perception concerning my warfare.**

Chapter 12
THE WARDROBE OF AN INFLUENCER

Influencer, if we're going to rule in multiple dimensions, rule the airways and effectively impact our spheres of influence, then as influencers we must understand that there are is an influencers' type of wardrobe we need to wear. Just as a police officer, or a Supreme Court Justice, even the soldier wears a uniform that makes them identifiable to what they do and the type of authority they have, so it is for the influencer. Without their uniform, they appear just like everyone else. But they are not. There is something uniquely different about what these uniformed people do and what they contribute to society. **It's time to understand your wardrobe.**

Ephesians 6:13-18 says, Wherefore take unto you the whole armour of God, that ye may be able to withstand in the evil day, and having done all, to stand. Stand therefore, having your loins girt about with truth, and having on the breastplate of righteousness; And your feet shod with the preparation of the gospel of peace; Above all, taking the shield of faith, wherewith ye shall be able to quench all the fiery darts of the wicked. And take the helmet of salvation, and the sword of the Spirit, which is the word of God: Praying always with all prayer and supplication in the Spirit, and watching thereunto with all perseverance and supplication for all saints;

The enemy doesn't fight fair, so as influencers, we must be certain that we have on the proper attire each day. In our case, it's our wardrobe of war.

The Wardrobe of War

1) **The Helmet of Salvation** - In the Greek, the word *helmet* means the encircled protection of the head. When we wear the helmet of salvation it causes our minds to be renewed continuously. Because the mind is a spiritual battlefield, it is impossible to have a victorious life in Christ or be an effective influencer. So the helmet of salvation surrounds the headspace. You must protect your headspace and stop allowing people to occupy valuable space in your head.

2) **The Breastplate of Righteous** – This piece of wardrobe covers the chest area. Roman soldiers considered this part

of the armor to be the most important because it covered the heart. The mind and the heart are synonymous to the enemy. If the enemy has access to your heart then he has your mind. *Keep thy heart with all diligence; for out of it are the issues of life (Proverbs 4:23)* and *For as he thinketh in his heart, so is he (Proverbs 23:7).* The breastplate not only covers the heart, but it also covers vital organs.

3) **The Belt of Truth** – This important piece of wardrobe protects the influencer from the enticer. The enticer is a spirit that lures the soul of men and seduces them into perversion. The enticer extracts every ounce of righteousness out of them. What does this mean? It means that you know better, but you refuse to do better. Influencer, you must ensure that your "belt" is on and that it is properly fastened. This belt of truth binds up fornication, pornography, incest, molestation, masturbation, homosexuality, adultery, sexual fantasies, and even nightmares involving incubus and succubus spirits (demon spirits that exaggerates your dreams and in in some cases, may even engage in sexual behaviors).

4) **Feet Shod with the Preparation of the Gospel of Peace** – Shoes can either make or break well put-together ensemble. *Psalms 37:23 says, that the **steps** of a **good man** are **ordered by the LORD**.* Influencer, every time you share the Gospel of Peace you also usher the Shalom of God (God's peace). Resolution, solutions, answers, and

comfort should show up when you show up and not chaos or confusion. The preparation of the Gospel of Peace isn't just referring to preaching the Gospel, but it refers to LIVING the Gospel more importantly.

5) **The Shield of Faith** – In the Greek, the *shield of faith* is described as a large door-shaped armor of protection. Based on this and through scripture, we can safely say that when you use the shield of faith it closes the door to the enemy; therefore, we can conclude that the shield of faith actually closes doors to anything that is not Holy Spirit.

* * * * * *

You are not only influencing the natural, but you are influencing the supernatural and any passage the enemy is attempting to enter through, you have the authority to cancel, close, or call off! **Say this: These satanic passages have now been shut down so that our daughters, sons, our grandchildren, spouses, our church, and the Body of Christ will never have to go through again!**

INFLUENCER PROPHETIC EXERCISE:

Allow the Holy Spirit to begin to reveal any areas of satanic passages and transmissions where the enemy may have used devices and gained access to your family or to your assignment(s). Begin to close every door and every opening. Seal every door with the blood of Jesus and the fire of the Lord. *Note: Don't be afraid to enlist the help of your Pastors, Elders, your deliverance ministers or leaders who specialize in this area of warfare if you need reinforcement(s).*

Now, influencer, start each day by applying your wardrobe of war.

It's time to change the world.

ABOUT THE AUTHOR

The ultimate INFLUENCER, Dr. Travis Jennings, a trailblazer, and 21st-century reformer, is an author, entrepreneur, executive producer, philanthropist, life-coach, husband, and father. Dr. Jennings has personally sold thousands of books globally. He's guided the careers and launching of other new authors and new entrepreneurs.

Apostle Jennings is also a highly sought-after orator who many will corroborate, that the status of their lives changed significantly after encountering his inspirational, revelatory, thought-provoking, and life-changing messages. He's produced several musical projects and has launched the careers of music artists, actors, and actresses or he's helped change the trajectory of their careers in some way.

Dr. Jennings has been honored by the state of Georgia, the city of Atlanta and the city of Lithonia for his philanthropic efforts. Dr. Jennings has overcome insurmountable odds. Along with his wife, he pastors a thriving ministry in metropolitan Atlanta. He has 5 beautiful children and one grandchild.

ADDITIONAL INFORMATION:

**Also available for purchase now by
Dr. Travis Jennings at www.theharvesttabernacle.org:**

Champions: It's time to Get in the Ring!

Life on Turbo

Lifeguard: Help is On the Way

Faith for the Gold

Contact information:

The Harvest Tabernacle
1450 S. Deshon
Lithonia, GA 30058
tsjbookings@gmail.com